BRITAIN SINCE 1930

Rosemary Rees
Sue Styles
Christa Hook

HEINEMANN
EDUCATIONAL

Heinemann Educational
a division of Heinemann Publishers (Oxford) Ltd
Halley Court, Jordan Hill, Oxford OX2 8EJ

OXFORD LONDON EDINBURGH MADRID
ATHENS BOLOGNA PARIS MELBOURNE
SYDNEY AUCKLAND SINGAPORE TOKYO
IBADAN NAIROBI HARARE GABORONE
PORTSMOUTH NH (USA)

First published 1992

**British Library Cataloguing in Publication
Data** is available from the British Library on
request.

ISBN 0 435 04363 3

Designed by Ron Kamen, Green Door Design
Ltd, Basingstoke, Hants

Printed in Spain by Mateu Cromo

Acknowledgements
The authors and publisher would like to thank
the following for permission to reproduce
photographs:

Barnaby's Picture Library: 8E, 9Q, 10D, 10M
Bodleian Library: 9G
British Airways/Adrian Meredith: 10K, 10O
Camera Press: 5B
Cinema Bookshop/Ronald Grant: 9J
Environmental Picture Library: 10E
Mary Evans Picture Library: 2w0
John Frost Historical Newspaper Service: 3G, 9L
John Frost Historical Newspaper Service/Val
Randall: 1E
The Girl Guide Association: 2wK, 9S
Greater London Photograph Library: 3D
Harlow Study & Visitors' Centre: 3B, 3C, 7B,
Hulton Deutsch Collection Ltd: 1F, 1J, 1M, 2wA,
2wF, 2wL, 2wM, 2pA, 6H, 9K, 10N
The Labour Party: 2pC
Leeds Design Consultancy: 7D
London Transport Museum: 10F
Magnum/Peter Manow: 6G
National Motor Museum, Beaulieu: 3F
The *Observer*: 6K
Robert Opie Collection: 1A, 2wI, 2wJ, 5J, 6E, 9A,
9B, 9C, 9P, 10G
Philip Parkhouse: 7A, 9H
Picturepoint Ltd: 8A
Popperfoto: 3H, 4D, 4F, 4H, 4J, 7C,
Jill Posener: 5I
Private Collection: 8B
Quadrant Picture Library: 10I, 10J
Raleigh: 9R
Redferns/M. Cameron: 6J
Roger-Viollet: 8C
Sony UK: 9N
Alan Thomas: 4A, 4C
Topham Picture Source: 1C, 1D, 1G, 2wC, 2pD,
2pE, 2pF, 4E, 4I, 5E, 6B, 6F, 8D, 9D, 9I, 9M, 9O,
10A, 10B, 10C, 10H, 10P
The Vintage Magazine Co: 9E
Source H on page 53 is reproduced
by permission of Penguin Books Ltd

Cover photograph: Topham Picture Source.

Every effort has been made to contact copyright
holders of material reproduced in this book. Any
omissions will be rectified in subsequent
printings if notice is given to the publisher.

CONTENTS

1 The Thirties: rich and poor

Source A

It is summer 1936. Stan and May Williams have been married for a year. They live in a new house in Barnehurst, Kent. Stan works for the General Post Office at its London headquarters. He goes to work each day by train. May does not go out to work. Stan does not want her to. He earns £5 a week, which is more than enough to keep them both.

Stan and May get up early. Stan has to catch the 7.35 am train to London. He has quite a long walk to the station, so he must not be late leaving home. This morning a letter arrived while May was frying eggs and bacon for Stan's breakfast. The letter is from Stan's cousin, Harry. Harry lives in Jarrow, a town in the north east of England. Harry writes that he is going to join a march to London. 'What is this all about?' Stan wonders.

SUPER 1933 HOMES

BARNEHURST PARK ESTATE BARNEHURST, KENT
Estate Office : Station Approach, Barnehurst, Kent.
Telephone : Bexleyheath 406.

9/6 WEEKLY £395 FREEHOLD

NEW IDEAL HOMESTEADS LTD
BRITAIN'S BIGGEST BUILDERS

Thousands of new houses were built in the 1930s. This is an advertisement for some which were built in Barnehurst, Kent.

May got up extra early today so that she could make a start on the washing. It is Monday, and Monday is wash day. It is raining, which means she will have to dry everything indoors. May cooks, cleans, bakes, sews, washes, irons and does the shopping. She keeps the flowerbeds in the garden tidy, but Stan mows the grass. She makes jam and pickles. She bottles the fruit and vegetables which Stan grows on his allotment. May wants Stan to buy her one of the new electric vacuum cleaners. He has just had a pay rise. Perhaps this year they will have a summer holiday in a hotel in Eastbourne or even Torquay.

The Williams Family

In this book you will read about the Williams family. You will also see pictures of them. They are not a real family. However, their lives are like the lives of ordinary people who lived in Britain between 1930 and 1980.

Stan and May in their kitchen.

Only rich parents could afford to send their sons to public schools. Often these boys went on to the universities of Oxford or Cambridge. Most of them got top jobs. They became lawyers, politicians, doctors, big businessmen and leaders of industry.

Girls from rich families usually went to expensive private schools. When most rich girls were about 18 they went to Buckingham Palace and met the King and Queen. They went to lots of dances. Their parents expected them to marry boys from rich families. Rich people owned over half the wealth of Britain.

Ordinary people did get to the top. A man called Ramsay MacDonald came from a poor family living in a Scottish fishing village. In the 1930s he was Prime Minister twice.

Source C

Visitors to Lords cricket ground, in London, on 9 July 1937. They were going to watch a match between boys from two public schools, Eton and Harrow.

Source D

Only rich people could afford to go fox hunting.

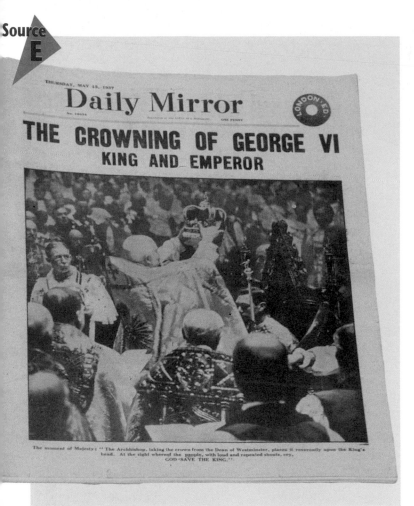

THURSDAY, MAY 13, 1937

Daily Mirror

THE CROWNING OF GEORGE VI
KING AND EMPEROR

The moment of Majesty: " The Archbishop, taking the crown from the Dean of Westminster, places it reverently upon the King's head. At the sight whereof the people, with loud and repeated shouts, cry, 'GOD SAVE THE KING.'"

A newspaper photograph of King George VI being crowned in Westminster Abbey on 12 May 1937. Thousands of people like Stan and May went to London and stood in the rain to cheer their new King.

In January 1936 King George V died. His eldest son was **proclaimed** King Edward VIII. King Edward wanted to marry an American, Wallis Simpson. Mrs Simpson had been married and divorced twice before. This meant that they could not be married in the Church of England. Mrs Simpson could not be crowned Queen of England.

In December 1936 King Edward decided to **abdicate**. He said his younger brother was to be king instead of him. Many people were shocked. Some said Edward should be allowed to marry Mrs Simpson and be king as well. Some said he should give up Mrs Simpson and stay king.

On 12 May 1937 Edward's younger brother was crowned King George VI. A month later Edward and Mrs Simpson got married. A new title was invented for them: the Duke and Duchess of Windsor.

Rich and poor

In 1936 1% of the British population owned over half the wealth of the country. Almost 75% of the British population could have sold everything they owned for less than £100.

The abdication

Stanley Baldwin, the Conservative Prime Minister, said that Edward VIII could not stay king if he married Mrs Simpson. Winston Churchill was the only Conservative MP who did not agree with him. Clement Attlee, the leader of the Labour Party, and most Labour MPs also thought Stanley Baldwin was right.

This family lived in one room in a house in Newcastle. All the food they had is on the table. The photo was taken in December 1938.

Couples like Stan and May weren't very rich but millions of people were poorer than them. Sometimes poor families lived in one room. They cooked, ate, washed and slept there. They did not have a bathroom. They washed in a basin or tin bath in front of the fire. They did not have an inside toilet. They had to go to an outside lavatory which was used by as many as 20 other people. Their houses did not have electricity. Their lights were gas lights or oil lamps. They cooked on a wood or coal fire, which also warmed the room.

Between April 1934 and March 1939 **local councils** had over 250,000 **slum** houses like these pulled down. More than a million people were offered new houses or flats to rent.

These new council flats were built in Wapping, East London, in the 1930s.

Unemployment was high in the 1930s. Everyone was afraid of being out of work. In the First World War (1914–18) many people worked in industries like ship building, coal mining and iron and steel making. These industries were in the north of England, southern Scotland, south Wales and Northern Ireland. Once the war was over these jobs disappeared. Hundreds of thousands of people were out of work. Some got jobs in new industries like electricity and car-making. These industries were in the Midlands and south-east England. But many could find no work at all. In 1933 nearly three million people were unemployed.

Workers took wage cuts rather than lose their jobs. Often they had such low wages that they could not afford to feed or clothe their families.

If there was a vacancy in the warehouse there would be as many as 100 men applying for it. I've seen men weep because they were out of work.

A retired West Yorkshire mill worker remembers in the 1980s what life was like in the 1930s.

Unemployment

Some regions of Britain had much higher unemployment than others.

The list below gives the percentage of people in different regions who had been out of work for over a year. The information was collected in the summer of 1936.

South-east	6%
London	7%
South-west	12%
Midlands	22%
North-west	23%
North-east	26%
Wales	37%

Industries like coal mining, ship building, cotton, and iron and steel had collapsed. These industries were mostly in the north and in Wales.

Unemployment 1928–1938	
1928	1.25 million
1930	1.75 million
1932	2.80 million
1934	2.25 million
1936	1.75 million
1938	1.80 million

Unemployment 1928–1938.

Life was hard for people who were unemployed. The government insurance scheme paid them some money for 26 weeks. Hundreds of thousands of people could not find work in 26 weeks. The government paid these people money which everyone called **the dole**. People only got dole money if government officials decided that they really needed it. These officials added up all the money coming in to a family. Even 3d a week from a son or daughter's paper round counted. Then the father's dole money was worked out. This was called the **means test**. Unemployed people hated officials asking about their family affairs. Most of the time they did not argue, because without the dole they would starve. Sometimes they organized **hunger marches** to show the rest of the country what was happening to them.

Source J

An unemployed man in Wigan, in 1933.

Source K

Mrs J's husband had been out of work for 14 weeks. Though she was breast feeding the baby, I found that all the food she herself had had yesterday was a cup of tea at breakfast time, and tea and two slices of bread and butter, provided by a married sister living near, at tea time. From the husband's unemployment pay of £1 0s 0d a week, 5s had to go to pay off a debt, 6s 3d for rent and only 8s 9d was left for food and fire.

A Health Visitor wrote this in the 1930s after one of her visits to a poor family. (Look at the Conversion Chart on page 64 to see what these amounts would be in modern money.)

Source L

Nothing to do with time; nothing to spend; nothing to do tomorrow nor the day after; nothing to wear; can't get married.

One of the characters in a novel called 'Love on the Dole' explains what it was like to be unemployed. This book was published in 1933.

'Despair'

Source J is a famous photograph. It was printed in the magazine *Picture Post*. It is often called 'Despair'.

Hunger marchers from Jarrow on their way to London in 1936.

Jarrow was a ship-building town in the north-east of England. In 1936 eighty out of every hundred men in Jarrow were unemployed. Two hundred of these unemployed men marched to London. Men like Stan's brother Harry joined the march. They wanted to show the rest of the country how much they needed work. Kind people gave them food when they stopped to rest on their way to London. Bishops blessed them. The Leicester Co-op mended their boots. The government in London did nothing to help them. When the men got back home they found that their dole money had been cut. The people of Jarrow did not begin working again until the shipyards began building warships to fight in the Second World War (1939–45).

How do we know about the past?

There are many people alive today who can remember the 1930s. They can tell us what they remember about life then. We also know about life in the 1930s from the many different sources which were made then. Here are some of them:

> pictures and photographs
> TV and radio broadcasts
> letters and diaries
> official reports
> games and comics
> magazines and newspapers
> houses and furniture
> trams, trains and cars
> clothes

Perhaps you can think of some more.

Having a lot of sources does not always make it easier to find out what really happened. Why do you think this is?

2 The Forties: war and peace

War

It is April 1941. May, her baby Janet, her mum Ethel, her brother Jack and Rags the dog are all squashed into the Anderson shelter in Stan and May's garden. They have been there for two hours. They can hear the drone of German bombers overhead. Sometimes the ground shakes as a bomb lands near them. They hope they will be safe. They hope Stan and May's house will not be hit. Fred, May's dad, stayed in the house when the air-raid sirens sounded the alarm. He got into the cupboard under the stairs. He thought he would be safer there.

Stan joined the army in 1939 when war broke out. He is fighting in the deserts of north Africa. Stan hasn't seen his daughter Janet yet. May is doing her bit, too. She joined the WVS (Women's Voluntary Service) in 1939 and helps people who have been bombed out of their homes. Her neighbour Ruby is working in a munitions factory.

Jack isn't allowed to leave his job and fight in the war. This is because the work he is doing is important, and may help Britain win the war. He works in a factory which makes ships' engines.

They all hope the raid will be over soon. They can then see what damage has been done and whether any friends or neighbours have been hurt or killed.

Source A

People took cover in Anderson Shelters to protect themselves against air raids.

The government gave away 2.5 million Anderson shelters. Each shelter was made from two curved walls of corrugated steel. These walls met at the top and were bolted to strong rails. The shelter was then sunk 1 metre into the ground and covered with earth. The door was made from steel. Anderson shelters could protect up to six people from everything except a direct hit.

May and her family in their Anderson shelter.

13

On 3 September 1939 people heard on the wireless that Great Britain was at war with Germany. Millions of people, like Stan, went to fight. Thousands of women were left to cope alone. They had to keep their families safe and well for as long as the war lasted.

The Germans bombed British towns and cities. The worst bombing was called the '**Blitz**'. It happened between September 1940 and May 1941. German bombers attacked London and other important towns like Coventry, Birmingham, Hull, Sheffield, Southampton, Manchester, Cardiff, Belfast, Plymouth and Bristol. The bombers usually came by night, when there was a '**bombers' moon**' for the pilots to see by. They sometimes made **daylight raids** as well.

Air Raid Precaution (ARP) wardens looked after people during and after air-raids. They called ambulances and fire engines. They helped dig people out of their homes. They made sure, too, that there was a **blackout** at night. Not a chink of light must be seen. Enemy planes must not be given a clue as to where to drop their bombs.

Many families had their own air-raid shelters. Public shelters were built in cities and towns for everyone to use. Some factories and offices built their own shelters. In London people slept at night in deep Underground railway stations. Everyone had a **gas mask** in case the Germans dropped gas bombs, but they never did.

Source C

The Elephant and Castle Underground station during the Blitz, 11 November 1940.

Source D

We didn't notice the war, really. The only bit of excitement was when a bomb dropped on Eldroth moor and killed five sheep.

Mrs Morphet from Yorkshire remembers in the 1980s what life was like during the war.

Source E

The hours dragged on as we waited for the inevitable bomb. The throb of the German planes, the bells of the fire engines. We were too frightened to move. Four adults, one baby, one dog. We huddled together waiting for death.

Jean Long remembers an air-raid on Coventry.

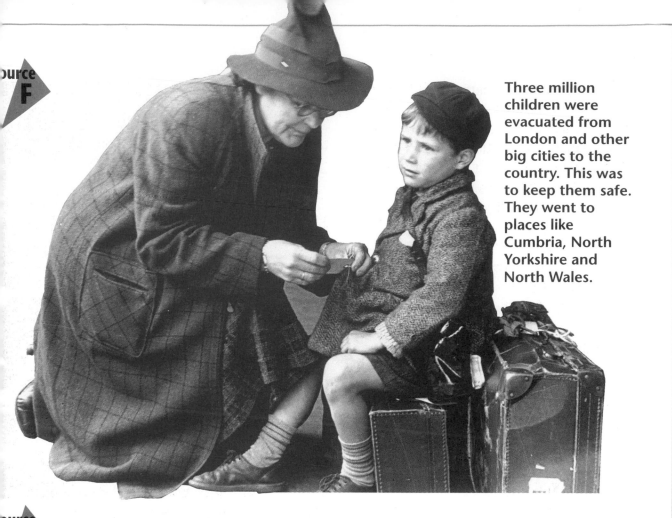

Three million children were evacuated from London and other big cities to the country. This was to keep them safe. They went to places like Cumbria, North Yorkshire and North Wales.

Everything was so clean. We were given face flannels and tooth brushes. We'd never cleaned our teeth until then. Hot water came from the tap, and there was a lavatory upstairs. This was all very odd. I didn't like it.

A boy, aged 13, writes about his evacuation.

Evacuation was the most exciting thing that happened to me. After school we were expected to work, sweeping out Mr Benson's butcher's shop. At home I never helped Father at his bank! In Settle I played in the fields and on the moors with village boys.

A boy, aged 13, writes about his evacuation from Bradford to Settle, in North Yorkshire, when he was 9 years old.

Evacuation and evacuees

The government made plans to evacuate school children and their teachers, mothers with young children and pregnant women. By 3 September 1939 nearly 1.5 million evacuees were living with complete strangers in country towns and villages. Some drifted back home after a few months. Over a million more women and children left the cities once the Blitz started in 1940.

Some parents sent their children abroad. They sent them to live with families in Canada and the USA until the war was over. Most parents, however, kept their families together.

Enemy submarines sank cargo ships bringing goods like beef, lamb, butter, wheat, oranges and bananas to Britain. The government rationed food to make sure the people didn't starve. Everyone had a **ration book** full of **coupons**. These coupons as well as money, had to be given to shopkeepers, for eggs, jam, cheese, butter, meat, bacon, milk, sugar, sweets, tea and soap. Some people were allowed more than others. Pregnant women had green ration books and got the first choice of any fruit and twice the egg ration. Children had blue ration books. They were allowed fruit, when the shops had any, and half a pint of milk a week. As well as coupons, everybody had 16 **points** a month to 'spend' as they liked on scarce food like tinned fish and macaroni. People got used to empty shelves and to queuing for everything.

People grew fruit and vegetables to help feed themselves and their families. Some of them had allotments. Others only had window boxes. Local councils dug up parks and playing fields. They planted cabbages, parsnips, potatoes, leeks and carrots. The government called this '**Digging for Victory**', and asked everyone to help.

Give yourself a HAPPY HOLIDAY...

...and help our farmers.

LEND A HAND ON THE LAN[D]

AT AN AGRICULTURAL CAM[P]

Farmers ploughed as much land and produced as much food as they could. They needed help to do this, especially at harvest time. Many people from towns and cities had farming holidays.

A typical week's supply of rationed food for one adult. Food was rationed differently at different times, depending on supplies.

A lot of things which people threw out as rubbish before the war were saved and re-cycled in the 1940s. Here, Girl Guides are collecting jam jars, rags, tins and paper.

Women like May tried to **make do and mend** during the war years. Clothes, towels, sheets, blankets and curtains were rationed. Everything unwanted or worn out was made into something else. They turned old sheets into baby clothes, net curtains into a wedding dress, flour sacks into chair covers and worn out trousers into girls' skirts. Nothing was wasted. They cut up old stockings and socks and used them as stuffing for pillows and soft toys.

Many people bought things on the **black market.** There was always someone who knew a man who would sell petrol, eggs, spare parts for a radio, toys or alcohol on the quiet. '**Spivs**' and '**wideboys**' ignored government regulations and sold whatever they could get hold of. Sometimes organized gangs stole goods from warehouses. Sometimes people **looted** bombed houses or shops, and kept or sold what they found there.

Rationing

In November 1939 people had to choose the shops from which they wanted to buy food like cheese, eggs and meat. They then had to register with these shops. In January 1940 everyone was given a ration book. They were only allowed to buy rationed goods at the shops they had chosen.

Rationing was important because it meant that everybody had enough protein and vitamins.

In May 1940 the German army reached the English Channel. People were very afraid that the Germans would cross the sea and **invade** Britain. The government told people to put huge concrete blocks and coils of barbed wire on the beaches. They told people to build look-out posts, called **pill-boxes**, along the cliffs. Farmers parked old tractors and ploughs in open fields to stop gliders landing. Vicars stopped ringing church bells on Sundays. Everyone agreed that church bells would only be rung to warn people that the Germans were invading.

Everybody got ready for an invasion, not just people living near the south and east coasts. Men who were not in the forces joined the **Local Defence Volunteers**, which was soon called the **Home Guard**. They trained to fight back invading troops. Women were not allowed to join. They formed the **Women's Home Defence Corps** instead, and learned to fire rifles and pistols too.

Source
L

Local Home Guard practising. At first they did not have proper uniforms or rifles. This photo was taken in 1940.

Source
M

Sign posts were taken away from road junctions so that invading Germans would get lost.

Source
N

We shall defend our island whatever the cost may be. We shall fight on the beaches, we shall fight on the landing grounds, we shall fight in the fields and in the streets, we shall fight in the hills. We shall never surrender.

Winston Churchill, the Prime Minister, said this on 4 June 1940.

You never know who's listening!

CARELESS TALK
COSTS LIVES

The government was afraid that people might give away secrets without meaning to. They published a series of posters called 'Careless Talk Costs Lives'. This one shows Hitler, the German dictator, and Goering, the chief of the German airforce, sitting behind two women who are gossiping on a bus.

What do people say about the past?

Wartime Britain was a terrible place. Cities were bombed and people were killed. Food was rationed.

The war didn't make much difference to some people. They didn't see or hear any enemy planes. None of their friends or neighbours were killed. No one starved. A lot of people ate much more healthily than they had done before the war.

'I shall tell the children that the war began in September 1939. I shall say how hard it was for people at home in Britain during the war. Their houses were bombed. They were short of food.'

Mrs Jones and Mr Smith are both giving their points of view about the war. They are also giving facts.

Why do people say such different things about life in wartime Britain?

'I shall tell the children that some people had a good time in the war. Some places were not bombed. Some people were not short of food.'

Peace

Hector comes home at the end of the war.

On 8 May 1945 the war in Europe ended. People hung up flags and banners. They sang, danced and had parties in the streets. Some parties were specially for the children. The grown-ups put tables in the road. They made cakes, buns and jellies. They cut sandwiches and blew up balloons. Everyone was happy because the war was over.

For some families the end of the war was a sad time. People they loved had been killed and would never come home.

Source B

6 June 1944	Invasion started in France at dawn. Did fractions – got on all right.
7 June	Went to Brownies. Had my bike out.
12 June	Mr Churchill went over to France. Mum not very well. Did biking.
19 June	Went to bed under the table. No warnings in the night. Can get off my bike properly.
22 June	Went to bed under the table. Eight warnings in the night.
19 July	Went to school. Warning went.
27 April 1945	Linked up with Russians. Had netball.
8 May	War over. Victory. Flag up. Bonfire.
12 May	Victory party in street.

Part of the diary of a ten-year-old schoolgirl, June 1944 – May 1945.

On 5 July 1945 there was a **General Election**. People voted for the **party** they wanted to govern Britain for the next five years.

The **Labour Party**, and their leader **Clement Attlee**, made lots of promises. They said there would never again be as many unemployed people as there were in the 1930s. They promised to build new houses for people who needed them. They promised to **nationalize** important industries and run them for the good of everybody. They promised to set up a **National Health Service** which would give everybody free medical treatment.

Many people thought the **Conservative Party**, and their leader **Winston Churchill**, would win the election. Churchill had led the British people through the war. Surely the people would want him to lead them in the peace which followed? A lot of people, however, remembered the unemployment of the 1930s. They remembered, too, that Britain wasn't really ready to fight a war in 1939. They blamed the Conservative Party.

Many people voted Labour in 1945 for the first time. The Labour Party won more seats in the **House of Commons** than any other party. There was a **Labour government**. Clement Attlee was **Prime Minister**. Most people thought the Labour Party would make the sort of Britain they wanted to live in.

Source C

THIS IS OUR CHANCE TO...

LABOUR

FOR HIM

VOTE LABOUR AND WIN THE PEACE!

LABOUR X

The Labour Party used this poster in 1945 to try to persuade people to vote for them.

War in the Far East

Fighting carried on in the Far East after there was peace in Europe. Britain agreed that the USA should drop atom bombs on Japanese cities. On 6 August 1945 the USA dropped the first atom bomb on Hiroshima; 70,000 people died. Three days later they dropped a second atom bomb on Nagasaki; 40,000 people died. On 14 August 1945 Japan surrendered.

In 1945 Britain was in a bad way. There were shops, offices, factories and houses in ruins. Docks were destroyed. Roads and railways were worn out. All these had to be rebuilt. The government had borrowed millions of pounds from other countries to help pay for the war. Now the money had to be paid back. To do this factories had to work again and make goods for **export**.

Source D

The Morris Cowley car factory in Oxford, in 1946. It aimed to produce 2,500 cars a week.

The new Labour government was very strict. They said car makers could only have steel if they made cars for export. They told new factories to open where there were lots of people out of work. They ordered **oil refineries** to be built. These refineries made petrol out of Arab oil, which was cheaper than USA oil. Refineries also provided raw material to make man-made fibres like **nylon**, **rayon** and **terylene**.

The Labour government believed that some industries were too important to be owned by individuals. They said that coal, iron, steel, electricity, gas and the railways should be run by the state. They **nationalized** all these industries. The government tried to make sure they were modernized and run efficiently.

Source E

More than 60,000 houses were built from 1945–46. Among them were 40,000 'pre-fabs' like these.

The Labour government said that it was their job to see that every man, woman and child in Britain was properly looked after. They ordered council houses and whole new towns to be built. They started a **National Health Service**, which gave free treatment to everyone. This was the beginning of the **Welfare State**.

Factories were rebuilt. Goods worth millions of pounds were exported. Money owed to other countries was paid back. There was very little unemployment. People earned good wages. There was, however, a problem. People had suffered a lot during the war. There had not been enough food, fuel or clothing. After the war rationing carried on. Even bread was rationed in 1946, something which had not happened during the war. Many people did not understand why. They saw goods they wanted to buy being exported to other countries. The terrible winter of 1947 did not help. Many people could not buy enough coal or food to keep themselves warm. In the General Election of 1950 the Labour government had a majority of just eight seats. There was another General Election in 1951 which the Conservatives won.

A Royal Wedding

On 20 November 1947 Princess Elizabeth, the elder daughter of the King and Queen, married Prince Philip in Westminster Abbey. People began to think that better times lay ahead for everyone.

Were things different then?

Source F shows horses pulling a plough. Most farmers now use tractors.

The photograph at the top of page 22 (Source D) shows a car assembly line. More jobs are done by machinery on car assembly lines today.

Source H on page 9 shows how many people were unemployed in the 1930s. Far fewer people were out of work in the 1940s.

At the end of the war, people celebrated; they

- danced and sang
- had parties
- lit bonfires.

Source
F

Ploughing during the terrible winter of 1947.

3 The fantastic Fifties

It is 2 June 1953. There are a lot of people in Stan and May's front room. They are all watching television. Stan has hired a set so that his family can watch the Coronation of Queen Elizabeth II. Not many people in their street have a TV. Jim and Ruby from next door, with their children Barry, Susan and Sheila have come to watch the Coronation too.

May has made tea and cut sandwiches for them all. Robert is already half-way through a bottle of ginger beer. Janet is thirteen now and goes to the girls' grammar school. She hopes the younger children will keep quiet. She doesn't want to miss anything. Her baby sister Alison will soon be asleep on Mum's lap, but Robert is six and can be very noisy. She saw Dad put a pile of comics – *Tiny Tots*, *Beano* and *Dandy* – behind his chair. Those will keep the younger ones quiet!

Source A

May hopes Stan will decide to buy the TV. There are some good programmes, like *Muffin the Mule* and *The Secret Garden* which Robert and Janet would enjoy. Stan would like the sport on Saturday afternoons. She would like to watch some of those new cookery programmes. A lot of food is not rationed any more. It would be fun to try new recipes.

The Coronation

People in cities, towns and villages all over Britain celebrated the Coronation. They held tea parties and organized galas, bonfires and fireworks. They planted trees and put commemorative wooden seats in parks. Children had a holiday from school. Their schools gave them coronation mugs, spoons or pencils. Manufacturers put pictures of the new Queen on things like china plates, biscuit tins, ice-cream cartons and pencil cases.

The Williams family and friends watching the Coronation on TV.

People desperately needed new homes. Houses were destroyed during the war. People were living in pre-fabs or with relatives. Many more were living in **slums**. The government, local councils and private builders worked hard. One plan was to build whole new cities out in the countryside. Jobs, schools and shops would be within easy reach of people's homes. Twenty new towns were built by 1961. People moved into them from the cities.

Shopping began to change. Usually people went to the baker for bread, the butcher for meat, the greengrocer for fruit and vegetables and the fishmonger for fish. Every shop had shop assistants who got the customers what they wanted. However, in 1950 the first **self-service** shop in Britain opened in Croydon. By the end of the 1950s, most large towns had a **supermarket**.

Source C

This is a kitchen in a house in Harlow, Essex, which was one of the new towns. This photograph was taken in 1957.

Source B

These are some of the new shops which were built in Harlow. This photograph was taken in 1953.

In 1944 Parliament made a law about children and schools. This law said that all children had to leave primary school when they were eleven. Then they had to go to a secondary school until they were at least fifteen. This would not cost their parents anything. Schools provided free milk at playtime. They had to provide lunches for everyone who wanted them.

Most children took an examination just before they finished primary school. This decided what sort of secondary school they went to. Some children were good at practical subjects. These children went to **secondary modern** school. Children who were good at subjects which needed a lot of reading and writing went to **grammar** school. About one child in every five went to grammar school.

This is a London primary school in 1958. Lots of new primary schools were built in the 1950s. Thousands more babies than usual were born after the end of the Second World War. This was called a baby-boom. Children like Robert were part of the baby-boom. By the 1950s all these children were old enough to go to school. New schools were built for them.

The green belt

London was growing bigger and bigger. More and more houses were being built.

The government said that this had to stop. They said that London should be surrounded by a ring of countryside at least five miles wide. Farmers could farm on the land. People could go there for walks and picnics. No one could build any houses there. This land was called the 'green belt'. All the New Towns were built outside London's green belt.

One summer holiday a lot of children got polio. Some were paralysed and some died. The council closed all the public swimming baths. They thought children caught polio at the baths. I remember cycling to our doctor's surgery. He gave me my first injection against polio. All my friends had injections too. It didn't cost anything. It was free because of the National Health Service.

Rosemary Dawson remembers the 1950s.

The Festival of Britain was held in 1951. It was a great exhibition of what Britain had done in things like science, technology and design. Most people felt hopeful about the future. They were right to be hopeful. In the 1950s most people had jobs. They earned more than ever before. People spent their money on **consumer goods** like fridges and televisions, and on cars and holidays. A British Prime Minister, Harold Macmillan, told everybody, 'You've never had it so good.'

Most young people who left school at 15 found a job. They earned good money. They wanted freedom. They wanted to show that they were different from their parents. Their parents didn't always approve. Many young people spent their money on clothes, records, cigarettes and make-up. They went to **coffee bars**. There they drank coffee and listened to **rock-and-roll** music from the **juke-box**.

Source G

This is from the magazine Picture Post Cheap holiday flights began in 1950. B 1958 two million British people were having their holidays abroad.

Source F

Economy and Quality that appeal to Everyone

This is a 1950s advertisement for Ford cars. Many people bought a car for the first time in the 1950s. This meant they could have picnics in the country and trips to the seaside.

Young people bought rock-and-roll records. They spent hours listening to them at home with their friends. They listened to American singers like Bill Haley and Elvis Presley, and to British singers like Tommy Steele and Cliff Richard. They **jived** to rock-and-roll groups and to **skiffle** groups. They went to rock-and-roll concerts and screamed when they heard their favourite singers.

The girls bought sloppy sweaters and trousers. They soaked their petticoats in sugar and water to make them stick out under their skirts. The boys wanted to look like pop stars and many of them tried to copy Elvis Presley's hair-style. Some boys wore long drape jackets, drainpipe trousers and shoes with thick soles. They were called **Teddy boys**.

Manufacturers realized that young people had a lot of money to spend. They began to design clothes and write magazines just for them. They began to make goods specially for them to buy. The word **teenager** was used for the first time.

Some people thought that they would have a better life abroad. Thousands of families left Britain to live in Canada, Australia and New Zealand.

How did things change?

Life in Britain changed a lot for most people between 1950 and 1959.

- Average weekly wages in 1950 were £6 8s 0d a week. By 1959 this had risen to £11 2s 6d.

- Twice as many people owned cars in 1959.

- Thirty times as many people owned TV sets in 1959.

- By 1959 chain stores like C&A and Marks and Spencer were selling fashionable clothes at prices most people could afford.

- ITV started in 1955; advertising showed people what they could spend their money on.

Source H

Tommy Steele often appeared on a TV programme called 'Six-Five Special'.

4 The 'swinging Sixties'

It is summer 1969. Robert is at the **pop festival** on the Isle of Wight. He is with his girlfriend, Linda. They are having a marvellous time listening to their favourite **groups** playing pop and rock music in the open air. Mum and Dad can't tell them to turn the sound down!

Robert is 22 and so is Linda. They were at **secondary modern school** together. Robert left school when he was 15. He went to **technical college** and trained to be a television engineer. He works for a local firm. One day he wants to have his own business. Linda works in a salon called 'Cut 'n' Curl' in the local **shopping precinct**. She is a hairdresser. They are saving up to get married.

Source A

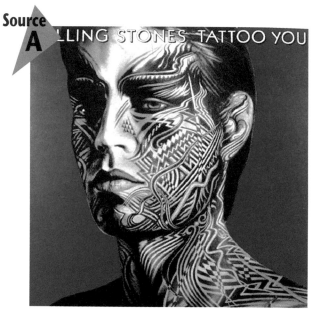

This is a record album by the 'Rolling Stones'.

Source B

May is worried. She hopes Robert and Linda will be all right at the pop festival. Alison wanted to go too. Stan and May said 'No'. They said she was only 16 and that was too young. Alison was cross. Some girls in her class at the local **comprehensive school** were allowed to go. Stan and May miss Janet. She was always so sensible. She is a nurse now. Last year she married Bill Evans, a doctor. They live and work in Bradford, West Yorkshire.

May works as a school secretary in the local primary school. May and Stan can now afford to have holidays abroad. They are saving money in the **building society** for when they retire.

Source C

This is a record album by the Beatles. In 1965 the Beatles were given the MBE by the Queen. This was because they sold a lot of records abroad and earned money for Britain.

Linda and Robert at the 1969 Isle of Wight pop festival.

People call the 1960s the 'swinging sixties'. For many it was a time for fun and a chance to be different. Britain led the world in fashion, design and pop music. Fashion designers, like Mary Quant, used new fabrics such as **PVC** and **plastic**. They had new ideas about what clothes should look like. Furniture designers used materials like **perspex** and metal. New furniture looked simple and un-fussy. People liked bold swirly patterns in black and white, or in bright colours like pink, purple and orange. Tourists poured into London, where exciting things were happening.

Some young people wanted a different sort of life. They were interested in Eastern religions and ideas. They believed in peace and love. They thought that caring about people was more important than making money. These young people were called 'Hippies' or '**Flower children**'.

This is a 1960s photograph of Mary Quant. She was a top British fashion designer. People all over the world bought her designs.

London was the fashion centre of the world. This was Carnaby Street, where people bought trendy clothes.

Television began showing programmes which made fun of anything which people thought was out of date. One of these programmes was called 'That Was The Week That Was'. 'Monty Python' was a crazy comedy programme which began in the 1960s. However, many people did not like this kind of thing at all. They preferred 'Coronation Street'. Huge numbers watched the broadcast on TV of Prince Charles being made the Prince of Wales. Plays shown in theatres were no longer **censored**. A play called 'Hair' shocked a lot of people because some actors were naked on the stage.

The Labour Government (1964–70) said that they wanted Britain to be a better place to live in. In 1965 Parliament said that no one should be **hanged** if they had murdered someone. Parliament passed laws, too, which let people live more the sort of lives they wanted to.

For many people the best thing that happened in the 1960s was when England won the football World Cup in 1966!

People often went on marches to protest against things they did not like. This is a photograph of a large demonstration in 1968 outside the American Embassy in London. People did not like American soldiers being sent to fight in Vietnam. In the 1950s and 1960s people joined CND (the Campaign for Nuclear Disarmament). They marched to protest against the nuclear bomb.

Agriculture

During the 1960s there were many changes in the way the land was farmed. Here are some of them:

• Farms became specialized. They concentrated on products like milk, or bacon, or wheat.

• Farmers used large expensive machinery. This meant that the number of farms fell and the size of farms grew.

• Farmers linked up with canning factories and freezing plants to produce what they wanted.

Me and my mates was really rooting for them. It was great when the final whistle went and then Bobby Moore held up the trophy. I felt proud to be English. I never thought England would win the World Cup.

Rob White remembers watching the World Cup on TV in 1966. England beat West Germany 4–2 in the final.

Not everyone in the 1960s was 'swinging'. For some people the 1960s were a time of sadness and worry. Programmes on TV made people think more about world problems. People gave money to organizations like **Oxfam** which helped starving people overseas. They supported **Shelter**. This set up projects to make slums fit to live in, and kept asking the government to provide houses for all who needed them.

Slowly, people began to realize that **pollution** from industry could harm all living things now and in the future.

The **churches** wanted everybody to understand the **Christian** message. In 1961 the **New English Bible** was published in modern English. It was soon a **best-seller**. However, fewer people went to church in the 1960s than ever before. The only church which increased its membership was the Roman Catholic church.

Source I

In March 1967 the oil tanker *Torrey Canyon* was wrecked off the coast of Cornwall. Giant oil slicks polluted the sea and the beaches. Birds and fish were killed. People tried to help, but no one knew what to do.

Source H

In October 1966 a great tip of coal waste buried a primary school in the village of Aberfan in South Wales. 116 children and 28 adults were killed. The rescue attempt was shown on TV. People were shocked and upset. They sent money to the disaster fund.

Source J

Immigrants arriving to live and work in Britain.

In the 1950s and for most of the 1960s there was plenty of work. There were even jobs which could not be filled. London Transport asked people from the West Indies to come and help run the buses and the Underground. Hospitals asked people from India and Pakistan to come and work as doctors and nurses.

Anyone who was born in a **Commonwealth** country could come and live in Britain. Many Commonwealth immigrants settled in the Midlands and the north of England, as well as in London. They brought to Britain new sorts of food, clothes, music and religion. Yet they were sometimes badly treated because of their skin colour. People already living here did all kinds of things to stop them getting jobs, renting rooms and living ordinary lives.

In 1962 Parliament changed the law to make it harder for Asian, West Indian and African people to come and live in Britain. Some politicians even said that only White people should be allowed to come and live in England. A lot of people were afraid that there would be **race riots**. In 1965 and 1968 Parliament passed laws which said that everybody, no matter what their colour or race, must be treated equally.

What do people say about the past?

Matthew is 17. He is talking to his cousin Tracey. She is 13.

> 'The Sixties were really awful. I don't think much of the clothes, or groups like the Beatles. Did you know that a coal tip in Aberfan buried a primary school and killed 116 children in 1966? And that in 1967 a big oil tanker was wrecked and polluted the sea?'

Tracey says to Matthew:

> 'The Swinging Sixties were really good! The clothes were fantastic and the music was great! Didn't you know that England won the football World Cup in 1966? And that 'Coronation Street' started in the 1960s?'

People say lots of different things about the 1960s. Some of the things they say are facts. Facts can always be checked to see if they are right. Some of the things people say are opinions. They are just giving their point of view.

5 The stormy Seventies

It is summer 1974. Janet and Bill have been married for six years. Their son Matthew is three. He goes to a **playgroup**. Janet and Bill are pleased that he will never have to learn about pounds, shillings and pence – only the new **decimal currency**. They all live in Bradford, West Yorkshire. Janet stopped work when Matthew was born. The local hospital sometimes asks her to help out when they are short of nurses. Bill works at a **health centre**. He is a family doctor. A lot of his patients are **Asian**.

Amar is one of Bill's patients. He is an **engineer**. Amar's parents chose a wife for him. This usually happens in **Muslim** families. They thought he would be happy with his cousin, Nasreen. Amar and Nasreen agreed. The families decided on a date.

Source A Janet at a Muslim wedding party.

The wedding was in Nasreen's house. Only the two families were there, with the **Imam** from the local **mosque**. The Imam read from the **Qur'an** and talked to Amar and Nasreen about marriage. Amar and Nasreen repeated three times that they wanted to marry each other. **Mahr** was paid to Nasreen and the marriage contract signed. The Imam blessed them, and asked **Allah** to bless them.

Amar and Nasreen then went to a marvellous party. All their relations and friends were there, including Bill and Janet. The men and women celebrated in separate rooms. Amar was the only man allowed to celebrate with his new wife and the other women. Janet hoped Bill was enjoying himself as much as she was! She wonders what Alison would make of it all. Alison has just finished studying at **Sussex University**. She has a degree in **Sociology** and wants to train to be a **social worker**.

Holy books

The Qu'ran is the Muslims' holy book. They believe it is the word of God. It teaches that everything that exists belongs to God and that people are the caretakers of God's world. The other important book for Muslims is the Hadith - reports of what the prophet Muhammad said and did. They are used by Muslim leaders today to guide their actions.

Source B

British troops in Northern Ireland.

There were terrible problems in Northern Ireland. The **Catholics** felt they had no chance of a fair life. This was because most people in Northern Ireland were **Protestants.** They ran the Northern Ireland Parliament and the local councils. The police were Protestants. Protestants got more and better council houses and jobs. In 1968 groups of Catholics began to say that they wanted things to change. One of their leaders was 21-year-old Bernadette Devlin. The Catholics marched and held peaceful demonstrations. The police tried to make them stop. Fighting began.

In August 1969 the British government sent soldiers to Northern Ireland to keep order. The Catholics hoped the troops would help them. Later they believed they were helping the Protestants. Some Catholics belonged to the IRA (the Irish Republican Army) which wanted to drive the British out and re-unite the north of Ireland with the Catholic south. Militant Protestant groups like the UVF (Ulster Volunteer Force) wanted to keep Northern Ireland united with Britain and to smash the IRA. It was hard for people living in Ulster not to take sides. In 1971 the IRA began to bomb shops, pubs and stations in England. They wanted to force the British government to talk to them. The government refused – but it could not stop them either. The violence is still going on.

Source C

We will fight for justice. If it becomes necessary we will simply make it impossible for any unjust government to govern us.

Bernadette Devlin wrote this in 1969 when she was 21 years old. She was an MP at Westminster from 1969 to 1974.

Source D

A week ago, one of our section commanders was hit in the stomach by a sniper's bullet. The locals cheered at the time.

A soldier wrote this about his time in Northern Ireland.

There were different problems in the rest of Great Britain. In 1973 petrol and oil were hard to get and very expensive. This was because of a war in the **Middle East** between the Arabs and the Israelis. Most of Britain's oil came from there. At the same time coal miners went on strike. Petrol stations closed. Power stations could not produce enough power for factories, shops, offices and homes. Industries worked for three days a week instead of five. Most people had electricity black-outs.

North Sea oil was pumped ashore for the first time in 1975. This was British oil. This made more jobs for some people. Even so, there were still serious problems. The goods produced by British factories cost more than foreign ones. More and more foreign goods were imported. British factories closed down and a lot of people became unemployed. Many of those who had jobs said they weren't paid enough. Some went on **strike**.

Source **E**

Nurses went on strike in 1979.

Source **F**

We have seen the grave diggers refusing to bury the dead; we have seen rubbish piling up in the streets; we have seen schools shut in the faces of children.

Lord Hailsham, a Conservative politician, said this in 1979.

Timeline: The seventies

1970   18-year-olds voted for the first time.

1971   Decimal currency introduced.

1972   'Bloody Sunday': 13 people shot dead by soldiers in Northern Ireland after a civil rights march.

1973   Britain joined EEC.

1975   First North Sea oil pumped ashore.

1976   Concorde started passenger flights.

1977   Queen Elizabeth II's Silver Jubilee.

1978   Wrecked oil tanker, *Amoco Cadiz*, polluted the English Channel.

Many people thought it was unfair that some women who did the same work as men were paid less. Women, and men who agreed with them, went on marches and wrote to their MPs and to the newspapers. They demanded **equal rights** for men and women. The government agreed with them. In 1970 Parliament said that women must be paid the same money as men if they did the same work. This did not solve the problem. In 1975, 25 out of every 100 people who went out to work were women. They earned a great deal less than men. Very few women had top jobs.

In 1975 Parliament said that women had to have equal rights with men when it came to things like education, getting houses, getting jobs and buying goods in shops. The government set up an **Equal Opportunities Commission**. This found out what had happened when a man or a woman said they had been treated unfairly.

Source G

A lot of people were very angry that I went back to work. They said I was taking a job away from a man who might have a wife and children. They said I should stay at home and look after the baby. They said my husband should keep me.

Karen Lancaster, on getting a job in 1977.

Source H

Perhaps the most important work of all is motherhood. If the good Lord had intended us all having equal rights to go out to work and to behave equally, you know He really wouldn't have created man and woman.

A male MP said this in 1977.

A woman added this graffiti to a poster for a Fiat car.

Source I

If it were a lady, it would get its bottom pinched.

If this lady was a car she'd run you down.

The beautiful 127 Palio.

FIAT

JLA 116V

There were some good times! In 1977 people celebrated the **Jubilee** of Queen Elizabeth II. She had been Queen for 25 years. There were services of thanksgiving, concerts and street parties. People rang church bells, held races, parades and carnivals. More than 100,000 people wrote letters to the Queen. In the same year Virginia Wade, a British tennis player, won the Women's Singles Championship at Wimbledon.

Source
J

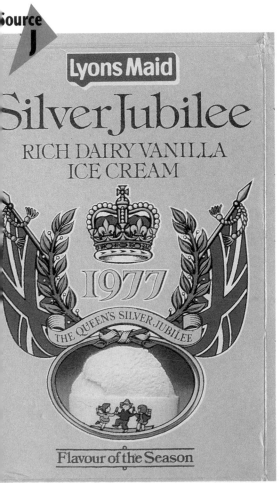

A Jubilee ice-cream carton.

Why did things happen?

In 1975 Parliament passed the Equal Opportunities Act. This Act made it illegal to label jobs as being for either men or women. It said, too, that women could not be discriminated against in any way.

How had it come about that women were legally equal to men?

- In the 1950s women worked in factories, as teachers and nurses, and in shops and offices. In almost every job women were paid at a lower rate than men.

- By 1965 women's pay in the Civil Service and teaching was the same as men's.

- In industry, the bosses argued that if they paid women more they would go out of business. The unions argued that equal pay would lower men's wages.

- In 1970 a new law said that men and women had to be paid the same if they did the same job. Many bosses just gave new descriptions to the jobs done by women, and carried on paying them less.

The Equal Opportunities Act was passed in 1975 because employers seemed to be getting round the law.

6 The Eighties: time for change?

It is summer 1987. Alison and Gavin live in a large Victorian house with their children Emily aged four, and Ben who is one. The house is in Camden, London. When they bought the house it needed a lot of repairs. It now has a new kitchen and two new bathrooms. It has new **wiring** and new floor boards. It has a new roof, with **solar panels** to save electricity.

Alison is a **social worker**. She helps families who have problems. Gavin is a **journalist**. He writes for a newspaper. He goes abroad and sends back reports from trouble spots. Anne-Marie lives with them and looks after Emily and Ben.

Tomorrow will be May's 70th birthday. There is going to be a family party. Stan and May are staying with Alison and Gavin specially for the party. Stan and May now live in Herne Bay, Kent. They bought a bungalow there when Stan **retired**. Janet and Bill are now divorced. She and Matthew are coming by train from Bradford. Janet helps run one of the hospitals there. Matthew is sixteen. He loves football and rock music. He hopes his cousin Gary, who is fourteen, does too, otherwise it will be a pretty boring weekend. Robert and Linda are driving from Barnehurst with Gary, Tracey and Lisa. Tracey is twelve. She likes horse riding. Lisa is seven. She has ballet lessons. Robert now has his own radio, TV and video repair business.

Stan and May are proud of Janet, Robert and Alison. They wonder what the future holds for Matthew, Gary, Tracey, Lisa, Emily and Ben.

Changes

Kitchens changed a lot between the 1930s and the 1980s. Look back at May and Stan's kitchen on page 5. Now look at Gavin and Alison's kitchen opposite.

In each picture, look specially for:

- the radio
- the sink
- arrangements for washing clothes
- what people are wearing
- what the men and women are doing.

Think about why these changes happened.

▶ **Alison and Gavin in their kitchen with Stan and Ben.**

The Conservatives, with their leader **Margaret Thatcher**, won the General Election in 1979. A Conservative government was in power all through the 1980s. What they did then changed the lives of everybody in the country.

Mrs Thatcher said that the government was to be involved as little as possible in people's lives. It was important, she said, that people did things for themselves. This is called **private enterprise**. Mrs Thatcher was a very determined Prime Minister and she usually got her own way.

The government cut the amount of money they gave to local councils. They cut the amount of money they gave for spending on schools, roads and **nationalized** industries. They stopped prices rising. The government said that people could buy their council houses. They said that nationalized industries, like gas, had to be sold to people who wanted to buy a **share** in them. The government cut **income tax** so that people could spend their own money as they wanted.

Source B

Margaret Thatcher was Britain's first woman Prime Minister. This is part of what she said when she was elected in 1979: 'Where there is discord may we bring harmony. Where there is despair may we bring hope.'

Source C

At last we've a house of our own. After years of renting we can now afford to buy. We feel that we really belong here now. No one can tell us to leave. It's our house, not the landlord's.

Jack Lord said this in 1987 when he and his wife bought a house for the first time.

Source D

For every £1 I earned I used to pay 33p in income tax. Now I only have to pay 25p tax. I've earned the money. Why shouldn't I keep as much of it as I can?

James Murray said this in 1990.

Source E

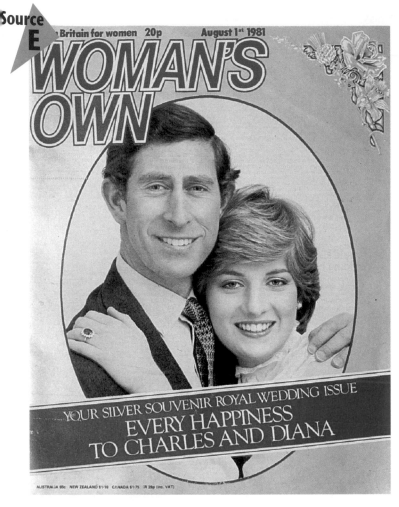

Britain for women   20p   August 1st 1981

WOMAN'S OWN

YOUR SILVER SOUVENIR ROYAL WEDDING ISSUE

EVERY HAPPINESS TO CHARLES AND DIANA

AUSTRALIA 85c NEW ZEALAND $1-10 CANADA $1-75 (IR 28p (inc. VAT))

The front cover of a women's magazine in August 1981. Prince Charles, the eldest son of Queen Elizabeth II, married Lady Diana Spencer in St Paul's cathedral on 29 July 1981. Huge crowds turned out to cheer them.

A year later their son, Prince William, was born. When Prince William was two years old, his brother Prince Henry (Harry) was born.

The eighties

1980   Unemployment: 2 million.

1981   City riots.

1982   Argentina invades Falkland Islands.

1983   Breakfast TV began. Unemployment: 3 million.

1984   IRA bomb hotel used by Conservatives for Party Conference.

1985   Anglo-Irish Agreement signed.

1986   Channel Tunnel agreement signed.

1987   Ferry sinks in Zebrugge harbour: 200 drowned.

1988   PanAm jet explodes over Lockerbie.

Source F

Information technology meant that good news and bad news were sent around the world very quickly.

The 1980s were not good years for some people. Many industries closed down or were in difficulties. In 1979 there were 1.3 million people unemployed. By 1983 there were over 3 million people out of work. Thousands of people, especially in the north of England, Scotland, Wales and Northern Ireland never found another job. There were riots in several large cities. Some people said this was because of unemployment.

There were other sorts of troubles, too. Many people were sad and worried by them. Many people were glad when the 1980s were over. They hoped that there were better times ahead.

Source G

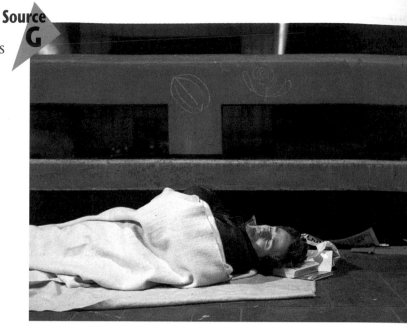

Hundreds of people slept rough on the streets of London and other British cities every night. Young people begged for money and food. Some people said it was their own fault they had no jobs and nowhere to live. Others said the government should do more to help.

Source H

On 11 May 1985 there was a terrible fire at the Bradford City football ground, where 51 people died. Football fans were also killed and hurt in violent accidents at the Hillsborough ground in Sheffield and at the Heysel stadium in Belgium.

Source I

It was April 1986. I was listening to the news on the radio. There had been a terrible accident in the Soviet Union. One of the nuclear reactors at Chernobyl had exploded. I knew what would happen. Clouds of radioactive gas would float over Europe. This would get into the rain which fell on the grass. The grass would be eaten by cows, sheep, reindeer and all kinds of animals. People who ate the meat and drank the milk from these animals could get cancer many years afterwards. I felt sad and depressed.

Sue Styles remembers in 1992 a radio broadcast she heard six years earlier.

Source J

There was famine in Africa. Men, women and children were dying. In 1985 Bob Geldof organized two huge rock concerts to raise money for them. The concerts took place in the USA and Britain at the same time. They were broadcast to 152 countries by the largest satellite link-up ever.

Source K

How do we know about the past?

The 1980s were good years for some people and bad years for others. There are a lot of sources which tell about the good times and about the bad times.

Sources C, D, E and F on pages 44 and 45 tell something about the good times. Think about which source shows what was best about the 1980s.

Sources G, H, I and J on pages 46 and 47 tell something about the bad times. Think about which source shows what was worst about the 1980s.

Do you think that historians will have problems in deciding whether the 1980s were good or bad for most people?

OBSERVER/HARRIS POLL

HOW HAS BRITAIN CHANGED OVER THE PAST 10 YEARS?

	%
Richer	48
Poorer	36
More freedom	44
Less freedom	24
More unhappy	48
Happier	21
More selfish	61
More generous	19

Opinion polls asked people what they thought. This poll was done by a firm called 'Harris' for the *Observer* newspaper in 1989.

7 Homes

Houses like this were built in the 1930s.

Houses

Source A shows a semi-detached house. There is another house just like this one joined to it.

Houses like this gave people living in them space for a garden and a garage.

Houses

Source B shows terraced houses. Terraced houses are joined to another house on both sides.

A lot of new towns were built in the 1950s. Harlow, in Essex, was one of them. These are some of the houses that were built in Harlow.

Source B

In 1968 a gas explosion did this damage to a tower block of flats called Ronan Point in London. People were hurt and some were killed.

Tower blocks were built in the 1950s and 1960s. They did not use up much land. A lot of families could live in them. However, people living in tower blocks faced lots of problems.

Flats

Source C shows a tower block of flats. Lots of families lived in them. Hundreds of tower blocks were built in Britain in the 1960s. Tower blocks did not use up much land, and so many were built. People who lived in them had to cope with lots of different problems.

Old houses in the middle of cities were often pulled down. Shops, offices and even tower blocks were built where the old houses had been. In the 1970s and 1980s people decided to keep the old houses. They did a lot of work on them. People lived in them again. These houses are in the middle of Leeds.

How did things change?

On these two pages you can see some of the different kinds of new homes people lived in between 1930 and 1990.

In some ways they are all similar. In some ways they are all different.

Some people moved into homes like these and their lives improved. Some people moved into homes like these and their lives got worse.

Do you think that people's lives would have got better or worse if they had moved into the homes shown in Sources A, B, C and D?

8 Clothes

Fashion

What people wore between 1930 and 1990 changed a lot. It didn't, of course, change for everybody at the same time. The table below shows the decades which each picture comes from.

A	B	C	D	E
1930s	1940s	1940s	1960s	1970s

Notice the change between the two 1940s pictures. One was from the war years and the other from peace-time.

Among the fashions you can see are:

- *A man with flared trousers and shoes with platform soles.*
- *A man with long hair, wearing a scarf and a wide belt over his hips.*
- *A woman in a jacket with 'square' shoulders and a shortish skirt.*
- *A woman wearing a long slim-fitting dress.*
- *A man in RAF uniform.*

Were things different then?

There were lots of differences between the clothes people wore in the 1930s and those they wore in the 1970s.

Source A shows the clothes a fashionable woman would have worn in the 1930s. Source D shows what fashionable teenagers would have worn in the 1970s. Remember, too, that in the 1930s some women wore trousers, and in the 1970s not everyone wore bell-bottomed trousers.

You can match the clothes in this Unit with the times the houses were built in Unit 7:

Source in Unit 7	Source in Unit 8
Source A	Source A
Source C	Source D

9 Spare time

Source A

Source B

Source C

Children read books and comics like these in the 1930s, 1940s and 1950s.

Children queued to borrow books during the war.

Source D

In the 1960s and 1970s magazines specially for teenagers were produced. There were magazines for children from Asia, Africa and the West Indies.

In 1967 a postal book club was started for children. It told them all about the latest paperbacks.

Some of the paperbacks available for children.

Libraries

Perhaps you have a library shelf or a library corner in your classroom? The books there are just for the children in your class. Perhaps your school has a library. The books there are for all the children in your school. Some may be too difficult for you; some may be for younger children.

Towns and cities have libraries. They have thousands of books in them for children and grown-ups. In country areas mobile libraries drive round so that people don't have to make long and difficult journeys to change their books.

In the 1930s almost half the people in Britain
went to the cinema every week. They saw
films like 'Top Hat' and 'Mickey Mouse'.

During the war most people listened to the wireless. They heard news of
battles. They heard programmes like 'ITMA' and 'Music While You Work',
which cheered them up.

Rhapsody

People bought transistor radios in the 1960s. 'Trannies' were small and neat. They didn't have to be plugged in to a power socket. They worked off batteries.

A lot of teenagers listened to pop music. Many teenagers listened to Radio Caroline. This was a pirate radio station. It broadcast from a ship. It played pop music all the time.

Source M

This teenager is listening to records on her own record player. Record players like this were made at the end of the 1950s.

Source N

This tiny television, 'Walkman' and CD player were made in the 1980s.

Radio channels

In the 1960s pirate radio stations began broadcasting pop music and advertisements. They broadcast from ships moored off-shore. The government found a way to close them down. Soon the BBC started Radio 1 as a pop channel. It also started local radio. As a result people had a greater choice of the sorts of programmes to which they could tune in.

Today there are lots of radio stations. Some are national, some are local. You could make a list:	
Station	Frequency

People on holiday at the seaside in 1935.

MONOPOLY
THE NEW GAME
AND THE
RAGE OF AMERICA
MILLIONS NOW PLAYING IT

The board game 'Monopoly' came from
the USA in the 1930s.

Meccano sets were often given to boys,
and sometimes to girls.

Source R

Boys and girls had 'Chopper' bikes in the 1970s.

Source S

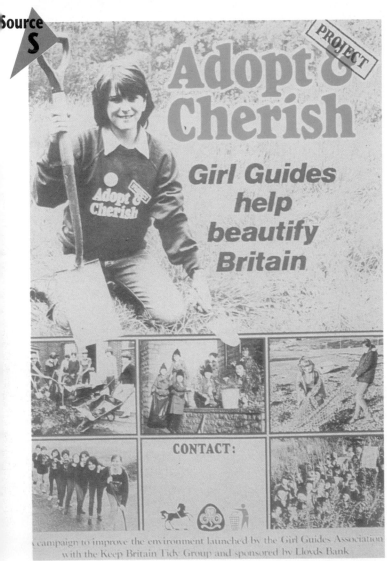

Girl Guides helped protect the environment in the 1980s.

How did things change?

All of the pictures in this Unit give information about some of the ways in which children enjoyed themselves between 1930 and 1990.

Some things changed a lot between 1930 and 1990; others stayed the same. Why do you think this was?

Think, too, about which things changed a lot and which things changed a little. Think about the reasons for this.

10 Getting about

Traffic on London Bridge in the 1930s.

Many city councils decided to stop using trams.

This woman is delivering milk in 1940. In some parts of Britain milk was delivered by horse and cart until the middle of the 1950s.

Motorways

In 1958 the first few miles of motorway were opened. This was a by-pass for Preston. The first 75 miles of the M1 were opened for traffic in 1959. A motorway network was gradually built over the whole of England. New bridges were built over the River Severn, the River Forth and the River Humber. Motorways mean that traffic does not have to go through the middle of towns. Motorways mean that traffic can move faster. They are only for fast, long-distance travel.

There were, and are, problems with building the motorway network. A lot of people had to give up their homes and land for the motorways to be built. People living close to motorways have to cope with terrible noise; other people found that motorways cut their communities in two. Motorway drivers face enormous 'tail-backs' if there is an accident or roadworks, and delays to their journeys. There are also many accidents in fog and ice because of the drivers' high speed. Is it worth it?

Source D

People bought cars like this in the 1970s.

Source E

A busy motorway in the 1980s.

BOOK TO
HAMPSTEAD
OR
GOLDERS GREEN
UNDERGROUND

People saw these railway posters in the 1930s.

SKEGNESS
IS SO BRACING

This is a photograph of Waterloo station, in London, in 1938. All these people are going on holiday.

A steam engine and carriages.

A '125' diesel
express train.

Trains

The sources on these pages show different sorts of trains. The grid
shows you the sorts of trains which people used for different sorts of
journeys.

Journey	Underground	Steam	Diesel
Going on holiday		✓	✓
Travelling in London	✓		
Travelling very long distances		✓	✓

This is an Imperial Airways flying boat. From 1936 flying boats like this one flew to Africa, India, China and Australia as well as Europe.

Flying boats

Flying boats meant that people could travel long distances. Not all countries had airports with runways. Flying boats could land on lakes, rivers and calm sea. They often landed in harbours.

This is the passenger ship the *Queen Elizabeth*. The *Queen Mary* was built in 1934 and the *Queen Elizabeth* in 1938. They were luxury ships. They carried passengers mainly between Britain and the USA.

This is a 1930s poster advertising the flying boats.

Source N

Jet engines were first fitted to passenger aeroplanes in 1952. BOAC (now called British Airways) fitted them to its new fleet of Comets.

Planes like this took people on holidays abroad in the 1950s.

Source O

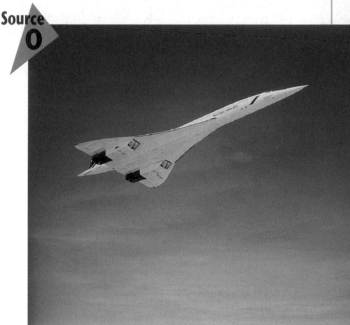

Concorde began making passenger flights in 1976.

How do we know about the past?

We know about the past because of the sources which were made then and which still survive. Look back at page 11 to remind yourself of what some of these sources are.

In this Unit there are a lot of sources to do with travel. These show us how people got about in past times. They can also tell us a lot more. Source L, for example, can tell us something about the way companies advertised. It can also tell us about the clothes people wore at the time. Look at the other sources and see what else you can learn from them.

Source P

A hovercraft at Dover in the 1980s.

INDEX

Conversion Chart

6d (sixpence) = 2.5p
1s 0d (a shilling) = 5p
10s 0d (ten shillings) = 50p
£1 0s 0d (240 old pence) = £1 (100 new pence)

Decimal coinage came in in 1971. Before then there were 12d in a shilling, and 20 shillings in a pound.

Comparisons: roughly speaking, sweets you could buy for 2d in the 1930s (such as a Mars bar) cost 6d in the 1960s, 6p in the 1970s and 20p by 1990.
